LAKE ERIE

A TRUE BOOK

by

Ann Armbruster

Children's Press®
A Division of Grolier Publishing
New York London Hong Kong Sydney
Danbury, Connecticut

Reading Consultant
Linda Cornwell
Learning Resource Consultant
Indiana Department of
Education

Subject Consultant
William D. Ellis
Editor of the quarterly journal
of the Great Lakes
Historical Society

Marshy waters at Point
Pelee National Park on
Lake Erie

Library of Congress Cataloging-in-Publication Data

Armbruster, Ann.
    Lake Erie / by Ann Armbruster.
        p.   cm. — (A true book)
    Includes index.
    Summary: Discusses the history, nautical stories, and industrial and
social significance of Lake Erie.
    ISBN 0-516-20011-9 (lib. bdg.)   ISBN 0-516-26102-9 (pbk.)
    1. Erie, Lake—Juvenile literature. [1. Erie, Lake.] I. Title. II. Series.
F555.A76 1996
977.1'2—dc20   96-2028
                                                                      CIP
                                                                       AC

Contents

Glaciers moved tons of rock to form Lake Erie and the other Great Lakes.

The Fourth-Largest Lake

Thousands of years ago, Ice Age glaciers covered the center of eastern North America. The weight of the glaciers moved huge amounts of sand and rock, creating deep valleys.

As the glaciers melted, some of the water stayed in the valleys and formed the Great Lakes.

Minnesota

LAKE SUPERIOR

C A N

O N T A R I O

N

Wisconsin

Michigan

LAKE MICHIGAN

LAKE HURON

Niagara Falls

Welland Ship Canal

LAKE ON

Niaga
Falls

Buffalo

Niagara
River

Chicago

LAKE ERIE

Illinois

Toledo
Put-in-Bay

Johnson's
Island

Kelley's
Island

Cuyahoga
River

Cleveland

Erie

Pennsylvani

Indiana

U N I T E D   S T A

Ohio

A D A

QUEBEC

St. Lawrence River

St.

Prince
Edward
Island

New
Brunswick

Maine

Nova Scotia

O

Erie Canal

Vermont

New
Hampshire

New York

Hudson River

Massachusetts

Connecticut

Rhode
Island

T E S

New Jersey

ATLANTIC
OCEAN

Lake Erie, Lake Huron, Lake Michigan, Lake Ontario, and Lake Superior are the five Great Lakes. Lake Erie is the fourth-largest of the group. It is also the shallowest. Its average depth is only 62 feet (19 meters).

Lake Erie is the farthest south of the Great Lakes. The states of Ohio, Pennsylvania, Michigan, and New York, and the Canadian province of Ontario touch its borders.

Niagara Falls

At its eastern end, Lake Erie
empties into the Niagara River.
This river connects Lake Erie to
Lake Ontario. About midway
in its course, the Niagara drops
326 feet (99 m) over two steep
waterfalls called Horseshoe Falls
and American Falls. Together,
they are called Niagara Falls.

The falls are on the United

Niagara Falls

States–Canada border between Niagara Falls, New York, and Niagara Falls, Ontario. More than 3.5 million tourists come to see them every year. On the Canadian side, tourists can watch 84 million gallons (320 million liters) of water plunge over the Horseshoe Falls every minute!

Some tourists watch the falls from above, safe and dry. Others get a close-up and wet view in the boat *Maid of the Mist.*

This cargo ship just fits as it passes through the Welland Ship Canal.

Early French explorers used the Niagara River as an inland water route. They made a route over land, or a portage, around the falls. Today the Welland Ship Canal bypasses the falls to connect Lake Erie and Lake Ontario.

Wavy Waters

Dangerous seiche waves (pronounced "saysh") frequently strike Lake Erie. Water in a seiche wave moves up and down. These waves may be caused by changes in the atmosphere. The force of a seiche wave is similar to that of a tidal wave at sea.

During a seiche wave on Lake Erie, the water rises at one end of the lake. At the other end, it can drop 8 feet (2.4 m) in three minutes!

Dangerous Waters

Navigation on Lake Erie can be dangerous. Its shallow waters can rise in steep waves without warning. Storms strike suddenly. The waters of Lake Erie have a dangerous reputation among sailors.

In 1818, *Walk-in-the-Water* was the first steamship to

Ever since ships have sailed Lake Erie, they have had to battle its steep waves and stormy weather.

appear on Lake Erie. The ship was named after an American Indian's description of a steam- boat on the Hudson River.

The smoke from *Walk-in-the-Water* was a common sight on Lake Erie.

Walk-in-the-Water was the first ship to combine steam power with sails. The wood smoke from the ship's stack was a familiar sight around the lake. The steam whistle had not yet been invented, so the boat crew fired a gun to announce the ship's arrival and departure.

In 1821, *Walk-in-the-Water* was caught in a severe storm near Buffalo, New York. The passengers were saved, but the ship was destroyed.

The passengers of *Walk-in-the-Water* were saved from the dangerous storm of November 1, 1821.

The Battle of Lake Erie

Lake Erie was the scene of a major battle during the War of 1812. This war was between the United States and Great Britain. Both sides were fighting for control of the entire Great Lakes region.

In Erie, Pennsylvania, on the shores of Lake Erie, ship-builders constructed ships for

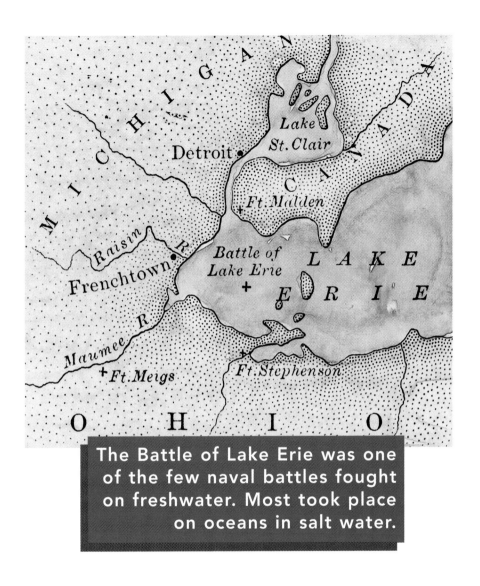

The Battle of Lake Erie was one of the few naval battles fought on freshwater. Most took place on oceans in salt water.

the battle. The task was enormous. Hardy frontiersmen used timber cut from nearby forests. They hauled heavy

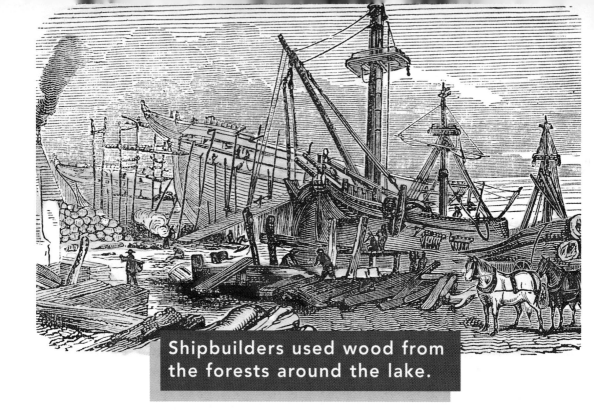

Shipbuilders used wood from the forests around the lake.

guns and cannon, rope for the ships' rigging, and canvas for the sails over long distances and rough roads. Finally, the ships were ready for the leader of the battle—Lieutenant Oliver Hazard Perry.

On September 10, 1813,

When Oliver Hazard Perry (left) saw the enemy, he declared, "We have met the enemy and they are ours." The *Lawrence's* flag held an important message (above).

Perry's fleet of ten ships challenged the British. His battleship, the *Lawrence,* carried the motto, "Don't give up the ship!"

In a few hours, the *Lawrence* was completely disabled. Most of the crew were dead. The daring Perry transferred to another ship, the *Niagara*, and sailed into the British fleet.

Captain Robert Barclay, heroic commander of the British fleet, was wounded, but continued to fight. Soon, the British suffered heavy losses

Even when the battle seemed lost, Perry jumped into a boat and transferred to another battleship to continue the fight.

Today, visitors can see a reconstruction of Perry's victorious ship, the *Niagara.*

and were forced to surrender.

After the battle, Perry was known as Commodore Perry. His victory gave the United States control of Lake Erie. The United States won the War of 1812 on both land and sea.

Ports

The Great Lakes are often called "inland seas" because of their large size. And, like seas or oceans, these lakes have ports. A port, or harbor, is a place where ships can anchor. Here, they are safe from storms. A port is also a place where ships load and unload cargo.

A ship drops its anchor in a Lake Erie port (left). Tons of cargo are loaded onto ships (below), and then are carried out to the Atlantic Ocean.

One of the major ports on Lake Erie is Cleveland, Ohio. Cleveland lies at the mouth of the Cuyahoga River on the lake's southern shore. It is located near the center of industrial America, halfway between Chicago, Illinois, and New York.

The skyline of Cleveland, Ohio

Cleveland in the 1830s

In 1830, the Ohio Canal
opened, connecting the Ohio
River and Lake Erie. Cleveland
then became Ohio's most
important shipping center.
The Erie Canal (opened in
1825) and the St. Lawrence
Seaway (opened in 1959) gave

An 1800s boat rides the Erie Canal, on its way to New York City.

Cleveland access to the Atlantic Ocean.

Erie, Pennsylvania, is another busy Lake Erie port. It is also Pennsylvania's only outlet on the lake.

Pollution

Water pollution has been a major problem on the Great Lakes. Pollution occurs when harmful substances enter the environment. Too much pollution can cause algae, a type of plant, to multiply in lake waters.

Lake Erie's shallow waters make it especially open to

Pollution, such as this from an oil refinery, was dumped into Lake Erie.

pollution. The deepest part of the lake is only 210 feet (64 m). By contrast, Lake Superior is 1,300 feet (400 m) deep and Lake Michigan is 900 feet (274 m) deep.

For years, industrial waste and untreated sewage from port

cities poured into Lake Erie. The Public Health Service reported that all major rivers to the lake were also polluted. In the 1960s, Cleveland's Cuyahoga River was so polluted that it caught fire!

When the oil on the surface of the Cuyahoga River caught fire, firefighters rushed to stop the raging blaze.

People worked together to make Lake Erie a cleaner environment.

Concerned citizens demanded action. In 1972, the government passed laws to help clean up the lake. Canada and the United States signed the International Great Lakes Water Quality Agreement. The pact provided joint goals for both countries to protect the waters of the Great Lakes.

Today, Lake Erie is cleaner. People enjoy the beaches.

Children build sandcastles on a Lake Erie beach.

A fisherman is ready for a catch (left). Walleyes (above) are known for their large eyes.

Sport fishing is popular. The lake is known as the "Walleye Capital of the World."

But pollution problems still exist. Watchful citizens and the government must cooperate to keep Lake Erie clean.

Sights to See

Kelley's Island is one of the largest of twenty islands in Lake Erie. Glacial Grooves State Memorial stands on the north side of Kelley's Island. Its limestone grooves are the largest of their kind in North America, carved by glaciers about 30,000 years ago.

Glaciers carved their mark on the rocks of Kelley's Island (left). Inscription Rock records North America's earliest history (right).

Another site on Kelley's Island is Inscription Rock State Memorial. Prehistoric American Indian drawings, showing human and animal forms, cover the large slab.

At Put-in-Bay, on South Bass Island, stands the Perry Peace

Monument. The 352-foot (107-m) structure celebrates Perry's victory on Lake Erie. It was built in 1913, the 100th anniversary of the naval battle. The monument also represents peace between Canada and the United States.

Guiding Lights

Lighthouses are tall towers with bright lights. The government builds them on the shore near dangerous waters to warn ships of possible danger.

Marblehead Lighthouse stands high on the lakeshore at Bay Point, Ohio. It is the oldest active lighthouse on the Great Lakes.

Marblehead was once a bea-

Marblehead Lighthouse (left) has guided countless soldiers safely home. The *Michigan* guarded the shores of Johnson's Island, where men were held in prison blocks (above).

con of hope to prisoners during the Civil War (1861–65). Thousands of Confederate soldiers were held on Johnson's Island in Lake Erie. They could see the light flashing from Marblehead.

Other Confederate soldiers tried to free the prisoners. They seized a steamship called the *Parsons*. But a Union gun-

boat, the *Michigan*, guarded Johnson's Island. Unable to challenge the Union cannons, the Confederates were forced to flee.

Another flashing beam across Lake Erie comes from Dunkirk Lighthouse. It stands at Point Gratiot, New York. This lighthouse once guided ships filled with immigrants who were looking to settle near the upper Great Lakes.

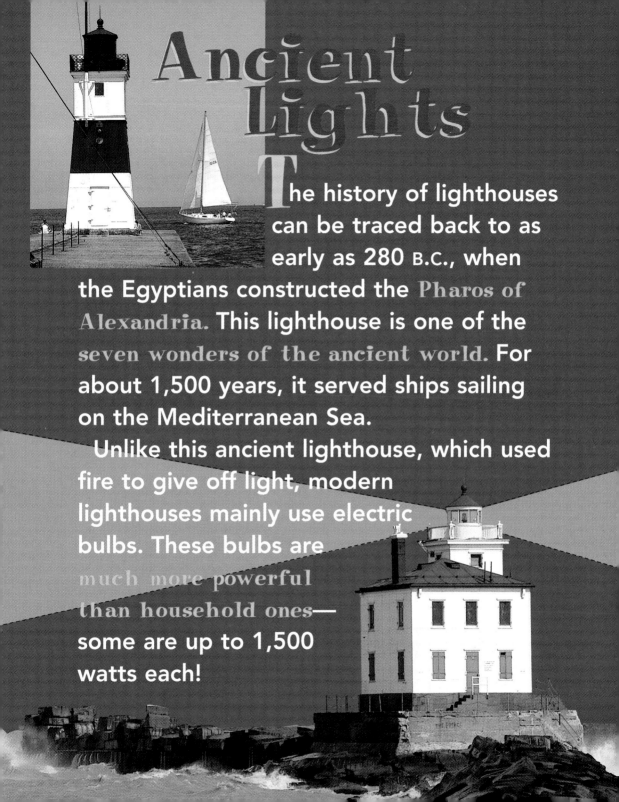

Ancient Lights

The history of lighthouses can be traced back to as early as 280 B.C., when the Egyptians constructed the Pharos of Alexandria. This lighthouse is one of the seven wonders of the ancient world. For about 1,500 years, it served ships sailing on the Mediterranean Sea.

Unlike this ancient lighthouse, which used fire to give off light, modern lighthouses mainly use electric bulbs. These bulbs are much more powerful than household ones—some are up to 1,500 watts each!

Lake Erie Today

After twenty years, much cleanup has restored life to Lake Erie. Ohio's governor now calls the lake "the state's most valuable resource." Lake Erie has made a comeback.

The port cities of Cleveland, Ohio; Toledo, Ohio; and Buffalo, New York, have rebuilt their waterfronts. Tourism is

booming. And Lake Erie, once the most polluted of the Great Lakes, is alive and well.

To Find Out More

Here are more places where you can explore Lake Erie and the states and provinces around it:

 **Books**

 **Organizations**

Brown, Dottie. **Ohio**. Lerner Publications, 1992.

Carter, Alden R. **The War of 1812: Second Fight for Independence.** Franklin Watts, 1992.

Nirgiotis, Nicholas. **Erie Canal: Gateway to the West.** Franklin Watts, 1993.

Zimmerman, Chanda K. **Detroit.** Lerner Publications, 1989.

Great Lakes Commission
400 Fourth St., ARGUS II Bldg.
Ann Arbor, MI
48103-4816
(313) 665-9135
glc@glc.org

Ohio Division of Travel and Tourism
P.O. Box 1001
Columbus OH,
43266-0101
1-800-BUCKEYE

Ontario Travel
Queens Park
Toronto, Ontario
Canada M7A 2E5
1-800-ONTARIO

Online Sites

Tour Lake Erie

http://www.great-lakes. net:2200/places/watsheds/ erie/erie.html

Uncover geographic and scientific facts, and ecological programs and organizations concerned with Lake Erie.

Discover Pennsylvania

http://www.great-lakes. net:2200/partners/GLC/pub /circle/penn.html

Explore Pennsylvania's 45 miles (72 km) of Lake Erie shorelines, its history, and its attractions.

Facts and figures about the Great Lakes

http://www.great-lakes. net:2200/refdesk/almanac/ almanac.html

Includes information about populations and the region.

Explore Lake Erie's shores

http://www.great-lakes. net:2200/partners/GLC/pub /circle/ohio.html

The 200-mile (322-km) Lake Erie Tour brings you to such places as Cleveland's Rock & Roll Hall of Fame, Cuyahoga Valley National Recreation Area, and the International Peace Memorial.

New York's Seaway Trail

http://www.great-lakes. net:2200/partners/GLC/pub /circle/newyork.html

Travel this 454-mile (730-km) route along Lake Erie, the Niagara River, Lake Ontario, and the St. Lawrence Seaway.

Important Words

bluff high, steep area near the edge of water

Confederate relating to the South during the American Civil War (1861–65)

fleet warships under one person's command

glacier mass of ice formed when snow piles up and does not melt

immigrant person who travels to a new country to make a home

mouth part of a river where it empties into a larger body of water

navigation steering a boat

rigging ropes that move a ship's sails

Index

Meet the Author

Living in Ohio, close to the Great Lakes, Ann Armbruster pursues her interest in history. A former English teacher and school librarian, she is the author of many books for children.

Photo Credits ©: Archive Photos: p. 12 (Frederic Lewis); Art Becker: p. 34 top left; Bettmann Archive: p. 21 top left; Buffalo & Erie County Historical Society: p. 13 top; D. E. Cox Photo Library: pp. 25 bottom, 37; Dossin Great Lakes Museum: pp. 16, 23, 25 top; Erie County Historical Society: p. 21 top right; George Stewart: pp. 6–7; Greenpeace: pp. 30, 32 both; Ian Adams: pp. 4, 13 bottom, 26, 41 bottom; Institute for Great Lakes Research: pp. 17, 36 top right; James P. Rowan: pp. 33, 40, 41 top left; Gamma-Liaison: pp. 10 (Joe Traver), 11 bottom (Andrew Klapatiuk); Mark E. Gibson: p. 43 top; New York Public Library Picture Collection: p. 27; North Wind Picture Archives: pp. 15, 19, 20, 22, 39 top right; Ohio Historical Society: p. 28; Photo Researchers: pp. 34 top right (Tom McHugh), 36 top left (Mark Burnett), cover, 39 top left (Bruce Roberts); UPI/Bettmann: p. 31; Valan Photos: pp. 2 (Stephen Krasemann), 11 top (Francis Lepine), 43 bottom (John Mitchell).